TABLE OF CONTENT

1. EASY FARMHOUSE LAMB STEW WITH VEGETABLES 5
2. CROCK POT PERSIAN LAMB STEW 5
3. ROSEMARY LAMB STEW 6
4. LAMB STEW WITH WHITE BEANS 7
5. CROATIAN LAMB/BEEF STEW WITH GREEN PEAS 8
6. CROCK POT LAMB STEW WITH BARLEY 9
7. AMAZING ONE-POT LAMB STEW 10
8. INSTANT POT CUMIN LAMB STEW WITH CURRY & CHILIS 11
9. LAMB RAGOUT 12
10. CHIPOTLE BEEF CHILI WITH LIME CREMA 12
11. BEEF CHIPOTLE CHILI WITH FRIED EGGS 14
12. FEIJOADA (BRAZILIAN BLACK BEAN STEW) 14
13. SLOW-COOKER BEEF SHORT RIBS 15
14. PORK TENDERLOIN, THE BEST EVER 16
15. PORK TENDERLOIN WITH BALSAMIC-CRANBERRY SAUCE 16
16. FRIED BREADED PORK TENDERLOIN 17
17. MOIST BAKED BREADED PORK CHOPS IN MUSHROOM GRAVY 18
18. BREADED BAKED PORK CHOPS 19
19. KITTENCAL'S ITALIAN BREADED BAKED PARMESAN PORK CHOPS 20
20. TUNISIA: BEEF MEATBALLS 21
21. ALL BEEF SWEDISH MEATBALLS 22
22. MONGOLIAN BEEF MEATBALLS 23
23. MOROCCAN BEEF MEATBALLS 24
24. BEEF MEATBALLS WITH REDCURRANT SAUCE 26

25.	SWEET PORK TENDERLOIN	26
26.	EASY SWEET PORK TENDERLOIN	27
27.	SWEET PORK TENDERLOIN WITH BACON LARDONS	28
28.	OREGANO & LEMON PORK KEBABS	29
29.	MARINATED PORK KEBABS	30
30.	QUICK & EASY PORK KEBAB	30
31.	PORK KEBABS WITH PINEAPPLE	31
32.	GERMAN STYLE GRILLED PORK KEBAB	32
33.	LEMON-GARLIC PORK KEBABS	33
34.	TERIYAKI PORK KEBABS	34
35.	BEEF KOFTAS	35
36.	LOW FAT MIDDLE EASTERN BEEF KOFTAS	35
37.	BEEF KOFTAS WITH MINTED YOGURT	36
38.	CURRY BEEF SHORT RIBS WITH HORSERADISH SAUCE	37
39.	SLOW-COOKED BEEF SHORT RIBS WITH RED WINE SAUCE	38
40.	BRAISED BEEF SHORT RIBS WITH A BORDELAISE SAUCE	39
41.	SMOKED BEEF RIBS WITH DEVIL SAUCE	40
42.	BEEF RIBS WITH CABERNET SAUCE	41
43.	BEEF SHORT RIBS WITH BARBECUE SAUCE	42
44.	VEGGIES & CHICKEN & VEGGIES	43
45.	PAN ROASTED CHICKEN & VEGGIES	44
46.	VA VOOM VEGGIE BURGERS	44
47.	EASY VEGGIE BURGERS	45
48.	COOL VEGGIE PIZZA	46
49.	PASTA WITH SAUSAGE, TOMATOES, & CREAM	47
50.	TURKEY BREAKFAST SAUSAGE PATTIES	48
51.	EGGS BAKED IN BACON RING	49

52. GREEN BEANS IN CHEESY BACON SAUCE (CROCK POT) 49
53. ASPARAGUS WRAPPED IN BACON 50
54. SLOW-COOKER BEEF SHORT RIBS 51
55. BEEF SHORT RIBS IN CHIPOTLE & GREEN CHILI SAUCE 52
56. CROCK POT BEEF SHORT RIBS 53
57. CURRIED BEEF SHORT RIBS 54

1. EASY FARMHOUSE LAMB STEW WITH VEGETABLES

Ready In:2hrs 15mins

Ingredients:11

Serves:4-6

INGREDIENTS

- 1 1/4 - 1 1/2 lbs lamb, stewing pieces (neck or shank or other meaty bits)
- 2 lbs vegetables, Combine ed (onion must be used, & add chop up bell peppers, zucchini, sweet potato, carrots & any bits you w)
- 5 tbsp flour
- oil (for frying)
- 3 tsp seasoning salt (BBQ, etc.)
- 14ozs tomatoes (1 tin, with juice)
- 1/2 tsp sugar
- 1 tbsp Worcestershire sauce
- 4garlic cloves, chop up & crushed
- 1hot pepper, seeds & ribs take outd, lightly chop up or 1/2 tsp Tabasco sauce
- 1/2 cup of dry red wine

DIRECTIONS

1. The vegetables you plan to use must be prepared, peel off, & slice into rounds or cubes. This has not been factored into the preparation time!
2. A thick layer of oil has been added to a hot big saucepan. The oil is well warmed.
3. Dip everypiece of meat in the flour that has been placed in a mini bowl while you wait. Don't worry if some parts are barely coated; just make sure the biggest pieces are.
4. To the heated oil, add. Make two batches of it. Add the remaining meat after one batch has sizzled on all sides & been pushed to the side of the saucepan with a long-h&led fork. THEY DO NOT ALL NEED TO BROWN.

2. CROCK POT PERSIAN LAMB STEW

Ready In:5hrs 15mins

Ingredients:14

Serves:4-6

INGREDIENTS

- 1 1/2 lbs lean boneless leg of lamb, slice into 1 inch cubes
- 1/2 tsp salt
- pepper
- 3 tbsp olive oil (separated)
- 2 big onions, thinly split
- 6garlic cloves, chop up
- 1/2 tsp dried oregano
- 1(14 oz) can whole tomatoes, drained
- 1 big potato, peel off & slice into 1/2 inch cubes
- 8ozs fresh green beans
- 1mini eggplant, peel off & slice into 1/2 inch cubes
- 1medium zucchini, slice int 1/2-inch slice s
- 5bay leaves
- 3 tbsp fresh parsley, chop up

DIRECTIONS

1. Half of the salt & pepper must be used to season the meat.
2. The lamb is cooked in a skillet over medium-high heat with 2 tbs of oil; once done, it is transferred to a 3 1/2-quart crock pot.
3. Cook the onions in the final tbsp of oil for 3 to 5 mins, or up to they are transparent. Cook & Combine the garlic & oregano for about a min.
4. While stirring, smash the tomatoes as you add them to the simmering pot.
5. About half of the tomatoes must be poured over the lamb in the slow cooker.
6. Season the potatoes with salt & pepper & arrange them on top of the tomatoes.
7. Green beans must be layered on top of the eggplant & zucchini.
8. To your liking, lightly season everylayer with salt & pepper.
9. On top, add the leftover tomatoes.

3. ROSEMARY LAMB STEW

Ready In:1hr 15mins

Ingredients:17

Serves:6

INGREDIENTS

- 1/2 lb lamb stew meat

- 1 big potato, peel off & cubed
- 1/2 onion
- 1/4 cup of flour
- 3 cups of hot chicken broth
- 2 tbsp olive oil
- 2 stalks celery, +some celery leaves, chop up
- 4 -6 mushrooms, split (non-compulsory)
- 2 tsp fresh rosemary
- 1/2 tsp fresh thyme
- 1/4 tsp oregano
- 1/4 tsp sage
- 1/8 tsp sea salt, as need
- 1/8 tsp black pepper, as need
- 1/2 tsp paprika
- 1/2 tsp Worcestershire sauce
- 2 tbsp red wine (non-compulsory)

DIRECTIONS

1. In a cooking pot, heat one tbsp of oil.
2. When the vegetables are tender & most of the liquid has been absorbed, add the onion, celery, & mushrooms.
3. Take out of the pot & reserve.
4. Add the meat to the pot after heating the additional tbsp of oil.
5. Cook in a skillet over medium heat up to browned all around.
6. The meat must be covered with flour & paprika before cooking for a few mins to lightly brown the flour.
7. Stirring while adding hot broth & scraping any particles stuck at the bottom (I use a wire whisk for this).
8. The meat must be Combine ed with the remaining ingredients, brought to a boil, & then simmered on medium-low heat for about an hour, or up to the flesh is tender.

4. LAMB STEW WITH WHITE BEANS

Ready In: 2hrs 20mins

Ingredients: 21

Serves: 8

INGREDIENTS

- 4 lbs lamb muster, excess fat & sinew take outd, slice into 1 1/2-inch cubes
- 1 1/2 cups of orange juice
- 6 garlic cloves, chop up

- 1piece ginger, 4 inches long peel off & grated
- 1 cup of fresh mint leaves, chop up
- salt & pepper
- 2 tbsp olive oil +more if needed
- 2 tbsp all-purpose flour
- 3 cups of beef stock
- 1 1/2 cups of dried navy beans, rinsed & soaked overnight or 3 cups of canned cannellini beans, rinsed & drained
- 8carrots, peel off & slice into 1/2-inch slice s
- 3bay leaves
- 2cinnamon sticks (3 inches every)
- 1 tbsp fresh oregano, chop up
- 1star anise
- 2 tsp coriander seeds, crushed
- 1 tsp ground cumin
- 1 tsp lemon zest, grated
- 2 tbsp lemon juice
- 2 cups of canned chop up tomatoes drained & slice into mini pieces
- fresh flat leaf parsley, to garnish

DIRECTIONS

1. In a sizable bowl, Combine the lamb, mint, orange juice, garlic, & ginger. For four hours, cover & refrigerate the marinade.
2. Pour the marinade-covered lamb into a col&er over a basin. Put the liquid aside. If you don't thoroughly dry the lamb using paper towels, the chunks will steam rather than sear. Season the lamb with salt & pepper as need.
3. In a big pot, heat the oil over medium-high heat up to it is quite hot. Working in three or four batches, fry the lamb pieces for 8 to 10 mins, stirring periodically, up to browned. Transfer using a slotted spoon to a bowl. Add the flour to the pot with the lamb once more, then whisk everything together. Pour the saved marinade in.

5. CROATIAN LAMB/BEEF STEW WITH GREEN PEAS

Ready In:1hr 5mins

Ingredients:11

Yields:4portions

Serves:4

INGREDIENTS

- 700g boneless lamb
- 250g onions
- 400g green peas (fresh)
- 200g potatoes
- 1 tbsp lard (or 2 tbsp oil)
- 2 tsp paprika (red, dried)
- 1/2 tsp thyme (dry)
- 1 cup of wine (white, dry)
- 3 cups of water
- 1 tsp salt
- 1/2 tsp pepper

DIRECTIONS

1. Make beef pieces that are 2-3 cm in size.
2. Onion must be lightly chop up & added to a pot with lard. Sauté onion up to it turns translucent & tender.
3. Sauté the meat after adding it up to it begins to release liquid.
4. Now whisk in the paprika, thyme, salt, & pepper.
5. Wine must be added & sautéed up to alcohol is gone. Cook for around 30 mins after adding some water.
6. Peel the potato & then chop it into little cubes while waiting (1-2 cm).
7. Shuck green peas, then take out them. Potato & green peas must be added to the stew & cooked up to all vegetables are tender & the liquid has been somewhat reduced. Severe heat

6. CROCK POT LAMB STEW WITH BARLEY

Ready In:4hrs 20mins

Ingredients:13

Serves:6

INGREDIENTS

- 1 1/2 lbs lamb stew meat, slice into 1-inch cubes
- 2 tbsp cooking oil
- 1medium onion, chop up
- 4garlic cloves, chop up
- 2 1/2 cups of low sodium chicken broth
- 1(14 1/2 oz) can diced tomatoes
- 1/2 cup of pearl barley (regular)
- 1/4 cup of dry white wine (non-compulsory)

- 2 tbsp chop up fresh dill or 1 1/2 tsp dried dill
- 1/2 tsp salt
- 1/4 tsp fresh ground black pepper
- 1(10 oz) jar roasted sweet red peppers, drained & thinly split (about 1 1/2 cups of)
- 1/4 cup of chop up of fresh mint

DIRECTIONS

1. A sizable heavy-bottomed pan or an electric frying device, as in my case, must be used to heat the oil. In the hot oil, brown half of the meat, then set it aside. When the beef is almost browned, add the remaining meat & onion. Add the garlic to the onion/meat Combine true & sauté for a few more mins after the onion is cooked, which must take around two mins.
2. The broth, undrained tomatoes, barley, wine (if using), dried dillweed (if using), salt, & black pepper must all be Combine d in a 3 1/2 to 5-quart slow cooker. Stir in the beef Combine true.
3. Cook with the lid on for 8 to 10 hours on low heat or 4 to 5 hours on high heat. Add the roasted peppers & fresh mint just before serving. If utilized

7. AMAZING ONE-POT LAMB STEW

Ready In:1hr 25mins

Ingredients:15

Serves:8

INGREDIENTS

- 4ozs bacon
- 2 lbs lamb muster
- salt & pepper
- 1 tbsp flour
- 1oz white onion
- 4garlic cloves
- 2 cups of dry red wine
- 2 tbsp paprika
- 1/2 lb button mushroom
- 4 cups of beef stock
- 1/2 lb canned canelli beans
- 1/2 tsp dried thyme
- 2bay leaves
- 3ozs carrots
- 1/4 cup of parsley

DIRECTIONS

1. Dice the carrots, chop the mushrooms, & mince the garlic & onions.
2. The lamb muster must be defatted & then chop up into bite-sized pieces.
3. Slice the bacon into pieces.
4. Render the bacon fat in a heavy-bottomed pan. Pour off any extra fat.
5. In the leftover fat, saute the garlic & the seasonings.
6. Add the lamb & brown in the pan.
7. For an additional 2 mins, add the cannellini beans, onions, & carrots.
8. Then, add the beef stock & red wine, & bring to a high boil.
9. Up to fork-tender, simmer for one hour.
10. Add salt & pepper as need.
11. To make a roux, Combine equal amounts of flour & butter. To thicken the stew, use this roux.

8. INSTANT POT CUMIN LAMB STEW WITH CURRY & CHILIS

Ready In: 1hr 20mins

Ingredients: 14

Serves: 4

INGREDIENTS

- 2 1/2 lbs lamb muster, slice in 1 1/2-inch cubes
- kosher salt
- 2 tbsp grapeseed oil, +more as necessary
- 1 big onion, slice lengthwise into 6 wedges
- one-inch piece ginger, skin-on, slice into thin slice s
- 1 head garlic, broken into cloves, skin-on
- 4 -7 whole arbol chiles, as need
- 2 tbsp ground cumin
- 2 tsp garam masala (or a combination of both) or 2 tsp Madras curry powder (or a combination of both)
- 1 tbsp cornstarch
- 2 tsp granulated sugar
- 2 cups of water
- steamed rice, for serving
- chop up cilantro, for serving

DIRECTIONS

1. Set the Instant Pot to the sauté position.
2. Salt the cubes of lamb well. Swirl in grapeseed oil after adding it to the saucepan. To avoid crowding the pan, add the lamb in stages & sear up to

brown, flipping once, about 5 mins per side. As they are done, transfer the lamb to a big dish.
3. Discard everything but 1 tbsp of the oil (or add an additional tbsp if pan is dry). Add the onion, ginger, garlic, & chile de arbol, season with salt, & cook for about 5 mins, or up to the Combine true begins to turn golden. Re-add the lamb to the pan. One more tbsp of grapeseed oil must be added, followed by the spices & a well in the middle. Stir to coat with oil & toast for 30 seconds or up to aromatic. Lamb & onions are folded in gently.

9. LAMB RAGOUT

Ready In:1hr 45mins

Ingredients:11

Serves:4

INGREDIENTS

- 1 lb boneless lamb, cubed
- 1 tbsp butter
- 1 tbsp olive oil
- 3cloves garlic, chop up
- 2 tsp lightly chop up fresh rosemary needles
- 1/2 cup of merlot or 1/2 cup of dry white wine
- 1(14 oz) can reduced-sodium beef broth
- 3 tbsp tomato puree
- 4roma tomatoes, chop up
- 1/4 cup of kalamata olive, pitted & chop up
- 1 tbsp chop up fresh parsley

DIRECTIONS

1. Over a high heat, brown the lamb with the butter & oil.
2. Add the rosemary & garlic, then stir for 30 seconds.
3. Stir in the wine before adding the beef broth & tomato puree.
4. For an hour, simmer on low heat with a cover.
5. As soon as the sauce starts to thicken, take out the cover & raise the heat to medium high.
6. Five mins later, add the tomatoes & olives.
7. Add the parsley & then serve.

10. CHIPOTLE BEEF CHILI WITH LIME CREMA

Ready In: 1hr 40mins

Ingredients: 14

Serves: 6-8

INGREDIENTS

- 3 lbs ground beef
- 3 cups of chop up onions
- 6 cloves garlic, lightly chop up
- 1/2 cup of chili powder
- 2 (14 1/2 oz) cans beef broth
- 1 cup of canned crushed tomatoes in puree
- 1/2 cup of stout beer or 1/2 cup of dark beer
- 2 tbsp chop up canned chipotle chills
- 2 tbsp yellow cornmeal
- 2 (15 1/2 oz) cans black beans, drained & rinsed
- 1 1/2 cups of sour cream
- 2 tbsp fresh lime juice
- 1 tbsp lime zest
- corn tortilla chips

DIRECTIONS

1. Over high heat, warm a heavy, big saucepan.
2. Add the beef & simmer for 8 mins, breaking up the meat with a spoon as it cooks.
3. Place in a big bowl.
4. Garlic & onions must be added to the same pot & sautéed for 8 mins or up to onions are soft.
5. Add the chili powder & cook for 3 mins, or up to aromatic.
6. Steak, broth, tomatoes, stout, & chills must be added.
7. Cover slightly & cook for about 1 hour & 10 mins, stirring frequently, up to the chili is thick.
8. Stir cornmeal gradually into the chili.
9. Beans are added after stirring.
10. Simmer up to thoroughly heated.
11. Use a lot of salt & pepper to season.
12. One day in advance, cover & refrigerate, then reheat over medium heat.
13. In a mini bowl, Combine the sour cream, lime juice, & lime peel.
14. Use salt to season.
15. Pour lime crema over the chili before spooning it into bowls.

11. BEEF CHIPOTLE CHILI WITH FRIED EGGS

Ready In: 1hr 20mins

Ingredients: 3

Serves: 2-4

INGREDIENTS
- 2 lbs lean ground beef
- sour cream (garnish)
- onion, chop up (garnish)

DIRECTIONS
1. Sauté beef & 2 cups of chop up onions in big Dutch oven over high heat up to beef is cooked through, stirring often & breaking up beef with back of a spoon, about 10 mins.

12. FEIJOADA (BRAZILIAN BLACK BEAN STEW)

Ready In: 26hrs

Ingredients: 9

Serves: 4-6

INGREDIENTS
- 1 lb dried black beans, soaked overnight
- 2 tbsp vegetable oil
- 1 big onion, diced
- 8cloves garlic, chop up
- 1/2 lb country-style pork ribs, slice in 1 inch peices
- 1 lb chorizo sausage, split
- 2bay leaves
- 6 cups of water
- cooked white rice

DIRECTIONS
- drain beans in col&er.

- in heavy pot heat oil, add onion & garlic, saute up to lightly browned.
- add pork & brown.
- add beans, chorizo, water to cover & bay leaf.
- simmer for 1 1/2 hours, covered.
- uncover, raise heat to medium, cook 15 mins up to thickened.
- salt & pepper as need, serve over rice.

13. SLOW-COOKER BEEF SHORT RIBS

Ready In:9hrs 10mins

Ingredients:14

Serves:6

INGREDIENTS
- 1/3 cup of flour
- 1 tsp salt
- 1/4 tsp pepper
- 2 1/2 lbs boneless beef short ribs
- 1/4 cup of butter
- 1 cup of chop up onion
- 1 cup of beef broth
- 3/4 cup of red wine vinegar
- 3/4 cup of brown sugar
- 1/4 cup of chili sauce
- 2 tbsp catsup
- 2 tbsp Worcestershire sauce
- 2 tbsp chop up garlic
- 1 tsp chili powder

DIRECTIONS
1. Fill a bag with flour, salt, & pepper.
2. Add the ribs, then shake to coat.
3. Butter-brown ribs in a big skillet.
4. Add to a slow cooker.
5. Combine the remaining ingredients in the same skillet.
6. Stirring as you bring to a boil.
7. Add to the ribs.
8. Cook on low for 9 hours with the cover on.

14. PORK TENDERLOIN, THE BEST EVER

Ready In: 1hr 35mins

Ingredients: 8

Serves: 6-8

INGREDIENTS

- 2 1/2 lbs pork tenderloin
- 1/2 tsp salt
- 1/8 tsp pepper
- 1 -2 tbsp flour (to dredge Tenderloin)
- 1 -2 tbsp olive oil
- 1(10 oz) box/pkg Lipton Onion Soup Combine
- 1(10 3/4 oz) can cream of mushroom soup
- 2 cups of hot water

DIRECTIONS

1. Set oven to 375 Ds Fahrenheit.
2. Slice the fat as much as you can.
3. Use salt & pepper to season.
4. Well-coated tenderloin is rolled in flour.
5. Cast iron skillet with olive oil on heat.
6. The tenderloin must be evenly browned.
7. Combine the heated water & the soups.
8. As much as possible, let the onion pieces rest on top of the tenderloin while slowly adding the soups to the roast.
9. After the inside temperature reveryes 170 Ds, bake the dish covered in the oven for approximately one hour & fifteen mins (well done).

15. PORK TENDERLOIN WITH BALSAMIC-CRANBERRY SAUCE

Ready In: 40mins

Ingredients: 7

Serves:2

INGREDIENTS

- 1 1/2 tbsp butter
- 1(8 -10 oz) pork tenderloin
- 1/2 cup of chop up onion
- 1 tbsp chop up fresh rosemary
- 1/2 cup of chicken broth
- 1/3 cup of canned whole berry cranberry sauce
- 1 tbsp balsamic vinegar

DIRECTIONS

1. set the oven to 450 Ds.
2. In a heavy, big ovenproof skillet set over medium-high heat, melt 1/2 tbsp of butter.
3. Put some salt & pepper on the pork.
4. Pork must be seared for 2 mins on all sides.
5. Put the skillet of pork in the oven.
6. Pork must be roasted for about 10 mins, or up to a thermometer inserted in the center reads 155°F.
7. Melt the final tbsp of butter in a big, heavy skillet over medium-high heat.
8. Add the onion & rosemary, & cook for three mins, or up to the onion softens.
9. Whisk in the broth, cranberry sauce, & vinegar for about 2 mins, or up to the cranberry sauce melts.
10. Place the meat on the work surface.
11. Add any liquids remaining in the big skillet to the cranberry mixture.
12. Simmer for about 6 mins, or up to sauce has thickened enough to coat a spoon.
13. Add salt & pepper as need.
14. Serve split pork with sauce.

16. FRIED BREADED PORK TENDERLOIN

Ready In:50mins

Ingredients:7

Serves:4-6

INGREDIENTS

- 3/4 - 1 lb pork tenderloin
- 2 eggs
- 1/2 tsp salt
- 1/4 tsp dried rosemary, crushed (I use LOTS more)
- 1 dash pepper
- 3/4 cup of dried breadcrumbs
- 3 tbsp vegetable oil

DIRECTIONS

1. Pork tenderloin must be slice into 1/2 inch slices.
2. pound to a thickness of about 1/4 inch.
3. 12 slices or so is about right.
4. Beat an egg with 4 tbsp of water, salt, rosemary, & pepper in a pie pan or medium bowl.
5. Spread wax paper with the bread crumbs.
6. Use tongs to dip the meat into the egg mixture to coat both sides, then roll it in the crumbs.
7. Continue coating every item twice.
8. Fry tenderloin up to golden on every side, about 5 mins per side, in hot oil in frying pan or electric skillet.
9. Up to all components are finished, keep warm.

17. MOIST BAKED BREADED PORK CHOPS IN MUSHROOM GRAVY

Ready In: 1hr 45mins

Ingredients: 15

Serves: 6

INGREDIENTS

- 6 pork chops (do not use fast-fry pork chops)
- 1 tsp seasoning salt
- 1 -2 tsp garlic powder
- 2 big eggs, beaten
- 1/3 cup of all-purpose flour
- 2 cups of seasoned dry bread crumbs (see Kittencal's Seasoned Dry Italian Breadcrumbs)

- 2 tbsp oil
- 2 tbsp butter
- MUSHROOM GRAVY
- 2(10 3/4 oz) cans cream of mushroom soup, undiluted
- 1(10 oz) can split mushrooms, well drained
- 3/4 cup of milk
- 1/3 cup of dry white wine (can use a few tbsp more)
- 1/2 tsp fresh ground black pepper
- 1 pinch cayenne pepper (non-compulsory)
- 1/3 cup of grated parmesan cheese (non-compulsory)

DIRECTIONS

1. Baking dish 13 x 9 inches, grease.
2. Use paper towels to pat the pork chops dry before seasoning with salt, pepper, & garlic powder.
3. The eggs, flour, & breadcrumbs must all be placed in separate bowls.
4. Over medium heat, melt butter & oil in a skillet.
5. Put the pork chops through a two-step dredging process: flour, eggs, & letting any extra egg drip off.
6. Finally, dust with seasoned bread crumbs.
7. For 4-5 mins on every side, or up to the breading is a light golden brown, cook the pork chops in heated oil.
8. Put the chops in the baking pan.
9. Wrap with foil.
10. oven to 350 Ds Fahrenheit.
11. Bake for roughly an hour.
12. Combine the cream of mushroom soup with the slice mushrooms, milk, white wine, black pepper, & cayenne pepper in a bowl in the meantime (if using).
13. When the pork chops have baked for an hour, cover them with mushroom sauce & top with Parmesan cheese.
14. When the chops are cooked, take out the foil & bake for an additional 25 to 30 mins.

18. BREADED BAKED PORK CHOPS

Ready In: 45mins

Ingredients: 9

Serves: 4

INGREDIENTS

- 4boneless pork chops
- 1 cup of Italian breadcrumbs
- 1/4 cup of parmesan cheese
- 1 tbsp oregano
- 1/2 tbsp sage
- 1 tsp rosemary
- 1 tsp cracked black pepper
- 1/8 tsp salt
- 4 tbsp butter or 4 tbsp margarine

DIRECTIONS

1. Turn on the 375 D oven.
2. In a big bowl, melt the butter & keep it warm.
3. In a sizable bowl, combine parmesan, seasonings, & Italian bread crumbs.
4. Dip the pork chops in the butter mixture, then coat them completely in the bread crumbs basin.
5. Depending on the thickness of the chops, bake at 375 Ds for 35 mins or up to browned.

19. KITTENCAL'S ITALIAN BREADED BAKED PARMESAN PORK CHOPS

Ready In:1hr 30mins

Ingredients:14

Serves:7

INGREDIENTS

- 2 eggs, lightly beaten
- 1/4 cup of milk
- 1 1/2 cups of dry breadcrumbs
- 1/2 cup of freshly gated parmesan cheese
- 1 1/2 tsp garlic powder
- 1/2 - 1 tsp salt (I use seasoned salt)
- 1/2 tsp black pepper (can use more)
- 1pinch cayenne pepper (non-compulsory)

- 1 tbsp dried parsley
- 1/2 tsp dried Italian seasoning (rubbed between fingers to release the flavor)
- 2 tbsp oil
- 1 tbsp butter
- 7thick-slice pork chops
- seasoning salt

DIRECTIONS

1. oven to 350 Ds Fahrenheit.
2. Grease a medium jelly-roll baking sheet or a 13 x 9-inch baking dish (or use a baking dish big enough to hold the chops in).
3. Eggs & milk are whisked together in a bowl.
4. Dry breadcrumbs must be combined with Parmesan cheese, garlic powder, salt, black pepper, cayenne, parsley, & Italian seasoning in a shlet dish.
5. Let the chops 45 mins or so to come to room temperature.
6. In a skillet, melt the butter & oil over medium-high heat.
7. Chops are dipped in an egg/milk mixture (leting any excess to drip off of the chops).
8. Completely cover with the breadcrumb mixture.
9. The chops must be browned in the skillet on both sides (for 4-5 mins every side), with seasoned salt sprinkled on both sides while cooking (you may omit this step if desired & just bake in the oven).
10. Put the object in the baking pan that has been prepared.
11. Cook the chops in the oven for approximately 25 mins (the cooking time will vary depending on how thick your chops are).

20. TUNISIA: BEEF MEATBALLS

Ready In:35mins

Ingredients:11

Serves:4

INGREDIENTS

- 1 lb ground beef
- 1 mini onion, lightly chop up
- 6sprigs parsley, lightly chop up
- 2 tbsp gruyere cheese, grated
- 2 tsp ground cori&er
- 2 tsp harissa (Tunisia)

- 1/2 tsp salt
- 2 medium egg yolks
- 1/4 cup of breadcrumbs
- 1/2 cup of mashed potatoes
- 1/4 cup of olive oil

DIRECTIONS

1. Directions Combine everything, excluding the oil. 10 meatballs must be formed. For about 5 mins, brown the balls on all sides in hot oil in a skillet. On paper towels, drain. Serve as an appetizer, over rice or couscous, or both.

21. ALL BEEF SWEDISH MEATBALLS

Ready In:2hrs 1min

Ingredients:15

Yields:32meatballs

Serves:8

INGREDIENTS

- 2 lbs ground beef
- 2onions (sauteed)
- 1/4 cup of butter
- 2 eggs
- 1/4 tsp salt
- 1/4 tsp pepper
- 1/4 tsp ground allspice
- 1/4 tsp ground nutmeg
- 2/3 cup of plain breadcrumbs
- SAUCE
- 1 1/2 cups of butter
- 1 cup of flour
- 6 cups of milk
- 1 cup of water
- 9beef bouillon cubes
- 2(16 oz) bags wide egg noodles

DIRECTIONS

2. Slice some onions & add some butter to a frying pan (sautee).
3. Combine breadcrumbs, eggs, salt, pepper, allspice, & nutmeg.
4. in the shape of a paste.
5. Paste, ground beef, & sautéed onions are combined.
6. Prepare balls, put them on a baking sheet, & bake them at 350 Ds.
7. for almost fifty mins.
8. THE SAUCE IS NOW:
9. Melt three sticks of butter in a big pot on medium heat.
10. Add a cup of flour.
11. combine, then warm.
12. adding slowly & stirring continuously Milk, 6 cups of (It must be making a thick white sauce).
13. Include 1 cup of hot beef broth (I use 9 Beef Bouillon cubes per 1 cup of water).
14. Stir continuously.
15. Let the gravy to begin to boil.
16. Stir continuously.
17. Off-heat the gravy.
18. The egg noodles require around 10 mins to cook. to them.

22. MONGOLIAN BEEF MEATBALLS

Ready In:55mins

Ingredients:19

Serves:4-6

INGREDIENTS

MEATBALLS

- 1 big egg
- 1 tbsp hoisin sauce
- 1 tbsp low sodium soy sauce
- 2 tsp grated garlic
- 1 tsp grated ginger
- 3scallions, lightly chop up
- 1 1/4 cups of panko breadcrumbs
- 1 1/2 lbs ground beef

SAUCE

- 1 cup of dark brown sugar
- 1/2 cup of low sodium soy sauce
- 1/3 cup of hoisin sauce
- 1 tbsp sesame oil
- 2 tsp grated garlic
- 1/2 tsp grated ginger
- 1/2 tsp red pepper flakes
- 2 tsp cornstarch

RICE & GARNISHES

- 4 cups of cooked rice
- 1/4 cup of split scallion
- 2 tbsp toasted sesame seeds

DIRECTIONS

1. For the meatballs, prepare a sheet tray with parchment paper & preheat the oven to 375 Ds F.
2. Using a fork, lightly beat the egg in a big bowl. Add the hoisin sauce, soy sauce, garlic, ginger, & scallions after that. The ground beef must be broken up into mini pieces before being added to the panko mixture.
3. Using a 1-tbsp ice cream scoop or spoon, form the mixture into meatballs & set them on the prepared baking sheet after thoroughly combining by h&. Round, smooth meatballs must be formed. Bake for 15 to 17 mins, or up to thoroughly done.
4. For the sauce, whisk together in a big skillet the dark brown sugar, soy sauce, hoisin sauce, sesame oil, ginger, garlic, & red pepper flakes. Bring to a simmer & cook for 6 to 8 mins, or up to the sugar dissolves & the sauce thickens.
5. In a mini bowl, combine the cornstarch with 1 tbsp water & stir up to smooth. Pour into the sauce that is already simmering, add the cooked meatballs, & heat for about 30 seconds, or up to the sauce has thickened & the meatballs are coated.
6. For the rice & toppings, arrange the meatballs over the rice & top with toasted sesame seeds & scallions that have been thinly split.

23. MOROCCAN BEEF MEATBALLS

Ready In: 45mins

Ingredients: 13

Serves: 4

INGREDIENTS

- 1/4 cup of olive oil
- 2 big onions
- 4 garlic cloves
- 1 egg
- 2 tbsp milk
- 1/2 cup of panko breadcrumbs
- 2/3 cup of chop up fresh parsley
- 1 tbsp chili powder
- 1/2 tsp cinnamon
- 1 1/4 lbs ground beef
- 16 ozs tomato sauce
- 2 tsp ground cumin
- salt & cayenne pepper

DIRECTIONS

1. Mince the garlic & chop the onions.
2. Spray cooking spray on a baking sheet with a rim & line it with foil.
3. In a skillet, heat the oil over medium-high heat. Onion & garlic must be sautéed for around 3 mins.
4. Combine the egg, milk, breadcrumbs, 1/3 cup of parsley, chili powder, & cinnamon in a sizable bowl. Combine thoroughly. Season the beef as need with salt & cayenne, then combine it with half of the onion mixture.
5. Place the 2-inch meatballs you've made from the mixture on the baking sheet you've prepared. Cooking spray must be used to coat the meatballs' tops. 6 inches from the flame, turn & broil up to all sides are browned.
6. To the remaining onion & garlic combination in the skillet, add tomato sauce & cumin. Over medium-high heat, bring to a boil while stirring occasionally.
7. Cooked meatballs must be added to the sauce. Once more, bring to a boil. Then, turn down the heat, cover the pot, & simmer for about 15 mins. While simmering, turn the meatballs every so often using a slotted spoon.
8. Add the remaining parsley over top. Over couscous or rice, serve the meatballs & sauce.

24. BEEF MEATBALLS WITH REDCURRANT SAUCE

Ready In:30mins

Ingredients:9

Serves:4

INGREDIENTS

- 1 lb lean ground beef
- 2 tsp dried oregano or 2 tsp marjoram
- 1 tbsp pitted black olives, lightly chop up
- 1 -2 tbsp sunflower oil
- 1pint prepared gravy or 1 pint hot beef stock
- 2 tbsp red currant jelly or 2 tbsp cranberry sauce
- 4 tbsp double cream or 4 tbsp creme fraiche
- 12 ozs tagliatelle pasta noodles (fresh or dried)
- freshly chop up sage leaf (to garnish)

DIRECTIONS

1. Combine the meat, seasoning, herbs, & olives in a big basin, then form the mixture into 12 meatballs.
2. The meatballs must be cooked for 15-20 mins, tossing them occasionally, up to the juices flow clear. Heat the oil in a big nonstick pan.
3. In the meantime, prepare the pasta as directed on the box/pkg.
4. Keep the meatballs warm after removal.
5. With just 5ml of oil remaining, add the stock or gravy & whisk in the cranberry sauce or redcurrant jelly.
6. Bring to a boil, then lower the heat, toss in the cream or creme fraiche, then lower the heat again & let the mixture simmer for a few seconds before adding the meatballs back to the pan.
7. Garnish the meatballs with sage leaves & serve with pasta.

25. SWEET PORK TENDERLOIN

Ready In:1hr

Ingredients:5

Serves:4-6

INGREDIENTS

- 2 lbs pork tenderloin
- 1/2 lb bacon, split thin
- 1 big onion, split thin
- 1/4 cup of soy sauce
- 12 -16 ozs apricot preserves

DIRECTIONS

1. Bacon-wrapped tenderloin.
2. At the bottom of a 9x13" casserole dish, arrange onions.
3. Over the onions, arrange the tenderloins.
4. Wrapped tenderloins must be topped with a mixture of soy sauce & apricot preserves.
5. Bake for 45 to 60 mins at 350.
6. Rice must be topped with split tenderloin & onions as a garnish. White rice is recommended.

26. EASY SWEET PORK TENDERLOIN

Ready In:1hr 5mins

Ingredients:2

Serves:4-6

INGREDIENTS

- 2 lbs pork tenderloin (Split)
- 10 -12 ozs jello with fruit

DIRECTIONS

1. Turn on the 375 D oven.
2. Place the pork tenderloin in the oven.
3. Slices must be spaced out such that every pink can be seen.
4. Fill a basin with empty jello containers & add fruit; combine up to mixture has the consistency of jelly. (I used three snack packs: one every of black cherry & pevery, but you can adjust the number to your preference.)

5. Spread jello over the top, cover it, & bake it for an hour.
6. The amount of servings depends on how the tenderloin is slice.

27. SWEET PORK TENDERLOIN WITH BACON LARDONS

Ready In:45mins

Ingredients:7

Yields:6Slices of pork

Serves:6

INGREDIENTS

- cooking spray
- 10pieces bacon
- 3 tbsp apple butter
- 2 tbsp honey
- 1/3 tsp ground allspice
- 1/4 tsp chili powder
- 1(3 lb) pork tenderloin

DIRECTIONS

1. Set oven to 325 Ds Fahrenheit (165 Ds C). Cooking spray must be used on a broiler pan.
2. In a big skillet, add the bacon. Cook, stirring occasionally, for about 5 mins, or up to the bacon starts to brown. In a mini bowl, combine apple butter, honey, allspice, & chili powder.
3. Four pieces of slightly cooked bacon are wrapped around the tenderloin & fastened with toothpicks.
4. The tenderloin is wrapped in the remaining bacon slices after half the apple butter mixture has been brushed over it.
5. Over the meat, spread the leftover apple butter mixture. On the prepared broiling pan, place the tenderloin.
6. Roast in the preheated oven for 30 mins or up to an instant-read meat thermometer inserted into the thickest section of the tenderloin registers at least 145 f Ds & the apple butter mixture has baked into a glaze.

28. OREGANO & LEMON PORK KEBABS

Ready In: 50mins

Ingredients: 12

Serves: 4

INGREDIENTS

- 1 lb lean pork loin, slice into 1 inch cubes
- MARINADE
- 1/2 cup of lemon juice
- 1 tbsp oil
- 2 tsp dried oregano
- 1 tsp rosemary sprig
- 1 garlic clove, crushed
- 1/4 - 1/2 tsp fresh ground black pepper
- CHOOSE 2 OR 3 FROM A SELECTION OF VEGETABLES
- 1 medium red pepper, slice into big chunks
- 1 medium zucchini, slice into 3/8 inch thick slices
- 8 grape tomatoes
- 1 medium onion, slice into big chunks
- 8 medium white mushrooms

DIRECTIONS

1. Combine all the ingredients for the marinade in a sealable plastic bag or non-reactive bowl.
2. Slice the meat into 1-inch cubes after trimming off all visible fat. Put the cubes in a bag & marinate them for 30 mins in the refrigerator. (If you'd like, you can also include the veggies. In particular, zucchini & mushrooms are excellent at soaking up flavor.
3. Wooden skewers are soaked in water in the interim.
4. For kebabs, wash & slice the vegetables.
5. Pork chunks & veggies are alternately woven into kebabs. You will need 1 big or 2 little skewers for every person, depending on the size of your pork cubes & the length of the skewers.
6. Cook for 8 to 10 mins on an indoor or outdoor grill.

29. MARINATED PORK KEBABS

Ready In:55mins

Ingredients:10

Serves:6

INGREDIENTS

- 1 1/2 - 2 lbs boneless pork loin
- 3/4 cup of cooking oil
- 1/4 cup of soya sauce
- 1/2 cup of vinegar
- 2 tbsp Worcestershire sauce
- 1 tsp dry mustard
- 1 tsp sage
- 1 tsp salt
- 1/2 tsp black pepper
- 1 garlic clove, crushed

DIRECTIONS

1. Split pork is used "& set them in a shlet pan.
2. The remaining ingredients must be incorporated well after being combined in a screw-top jar.
3. Put the pork in the marinade.
4. For several hours, cover & chill, occasionally turning.
5. Meat must be drained, dried, & skewered.
6. Warm up any leftover marinade to brush on the kebabs while they cook.
7. Slowly broil 5 "for roughly 25 mins. from embers.
8. During cooking, turn the skewers often & baste with marinade.
9. This is also a way to serve vegetables.
10. On skewers, arrange apple, green pepper, onion wedges, or mushrooms. Brush with marinade.
11. For 15 to 20 mins, broil.

30. QUICK & EASY PORK KEBAB

Ready In:50mins

Ingredients:13

Serves:4

INGREDIENTS

- 1kg pork muster
- 1 garlic clove, crushed
- 1sprig rosemary
- 100ml olive oil
- 1lemon juice
- combineed salad green
- 1red onion, lightly split
- 1tomatoes, lightly split
- 1/2cucumber, lightly split
- 150g tzatziki
- 1 tsp lemon juice (as need)
- 4pita breads
- 150g hummus

DIRECTIONS

1. Oven: Preheat to 180°C/gas 4. The pork fillet is seared in a preheated roasting pan. After seasoning, turn off the heat. Olive oil, rosemary, garlic, & lemon juice are added. Roast for 25 mins in the oven. Take out & take a 10-min break. slice meat thinly. It can also be barbecued.
2. Put the greens, onion, tomato, & cucumber in a big bowl for the salad. Combine thoroughly after adding the tzatziki & a squeeze of lemon juice.
3. By softly soaking & then lightly oiling every side of the pitas, they are warmed. Put in a frying pan & gently cook both sides.
4. Slice a hole in the pitta's top & spread some hummus inside. Then put the pork & salad mixture into the pita. Slice every ptta in half to serve.

31. PORK KEBABS WITH PINEAPPLE

Ready In:40mins

Ingredients:10

Serves:4

INGREDIENTS

- 1/4 cup of olive oil

- 3 garlic cloves, chop up
- 2 tbsp soy sauce
- salt & black pepper, as need
- 2 lbs boneless center slice pork chops, thick chops slice into 1-1/4-inch cubes
- 1 big fresh pineapple, slice into 1-inch chunks
- 2 red bell peppers, slice into 1-inch pieces
- 1 red onion, slice into 1-inch pieces
- 2 tbsp olive oil
- salt & black pepper, as need

DIRECTIONS

1. In a medium bowl, combine 1/4 cup of oil, garlic, soy sauce, salt, & black pepper.
2. Pork must be added & coated.
3. 30 mins to 4 hours are suitable for marinating.
4. In a another bowl, combine the pineapple, peppers, & onion with 2 tbsp of the olive oil. Add salt & black pepper as need.
5. Eight skewers are threaded with red pepper, onion, pineapple, & then meat. Continue up to every piece has been used.
6. Use the leftover marinade to brush.
7. Kebabs must be grilled for about 10 mins on a high heat, rotating once, up to the pork is thoroughly browned & cooked.

32. GERMAN STYLE GRILLED PORK KEBAB

Ready In: 1hr 5mins

Ingredients: 12

Yields: 12 kebab skewers

Serves: 3

INGREDIENTS

- 6 slices pork belly, about 1/2 an inch thick slice into long thin pieces or
- 1 lb pork muster, slice into 1/2 inch thick long thin pieces
- SPICE COMBINE
- 2 tsp salt
- 1/4 tsp fresh black pepper
- 1/2 tsp paprika

- 1/8 tsp curry powder
- 1/8 tsp cayenne pepper
- 1 tbsp oregano
- 2 bay leaves, ground in a mortar
- 1/8 tsp thyme
- 1/8 tsp garlic powder
- olive oil, extra virgin

DIRECTIONS

1. Add the olive oil after combining all the spices & let them to sit for a while.
2. Extra food can be placed in a canning jar & preserved for a very long period.
3. Spiralize the pork belly around the wooden skewer. Instead, you might pierce the slices in the centre. Before you wrap the pork over the wood skewers, let them soak in water.
4. Add the spice mixture in olive oil to the skewered meat.
5. Putting the prepared skewer in the fridge for one to four hours is non-compulsory.
6. Place the wood skewers on the grill & turn them once every min up to they are cooked to your preference. No more than five mins must be needed. If you prefer a stronger flavor, you can add more olive oil marinade while the food is being grilled, although it is typically not necessary.

33. LEMON-GARLIC PORK KEBABS

Ready In: 30mins

Ingredients: 5

Serves: 8

INGREDIENTS

- 2 lbs boneless pork loin, slice in 1.5-inch cubes
- olive oil
- MARINADE
- 1/3 cup of lemon juice
- 1 tbsp chop up garlic
- 1/2 tsp dried rosemary, cut up

DIRECTIONS

1. Put the marinade ingredients in a zipper-closed plastic bag.
2. Pork cubes must be added. The marinating time must not exceed six hours.
3. Skewer meat onto the sticks. Use olive oil to brush.
4. 7-10 mins on every side, or up to well browned & just about done, on a medium-low grill or broiler. Avoid overcooking to avoid harsh, dry results.

34. TERIYAKI PORK KEBABS

Ready In:20mins

Ingredients11

Serves:4

INGREDIENTS

- 1 1/4 lbs pork loin roast, slice into cubes
- MARINADE
- 1/4 cup of tamari
- 2 tbsp honey
- 2 tbsp sherry wine
- 1/2 tsp sesame oil
- 1 garlic, chop up
- 1/4inch piece fresh gingerroot, peel off & slice 1/4-inch thick
- KEBAB FRUIT & VEGETABLES
- 8pieces pineapple, 8 cubes
- 8shiitake mushrooms, stemmed
- 4green onions, slice into 2 2-inch lengths
- 8pieces red peppers, 8 cubes

DIRECTIONS

1. Tamari, honey, sherry, sesame oil, garlic, & ginger root must all be combined in a zip-top bag for marinating. Pork cubes must be added & coated. Turn the pork cubes at least once while covering & chilling for several hours or overnight.
2. Take the pork out of the zip-top bag.
3. On metal skewers, alternately thread chunks of pork, pineapple, mushrooms, green onions, & red pepper.
4. Heat the grill.
5. Put skewers on grill; cook covered for 8-9 mins, turning skewers every three mins, coating with marinade for the final six mins of cooking.

35. BEEF KOFTAS

Ready In:25mins

Ingredients:9

Serves:6

INGREDIENTS

- 2 lbs ground beef
- 2onions, chop up
- 1slice soft bread
- 1/2 cup of milk
- salt, pepper
- 1/2 tsp cumin
- 1/4 tsp chili powder
- 1pinch allspice
- 6bamboo skewers (or metal)

DIRECTIONS

1. Use bamboo skewers only after soaking them in water for at least an hour.
2. If possible, grind the beef & onions twice in a mixer. If you don't have a grinder, lightly chop the onion in a mixer first, then add the meat & pulse again up to the mixture is quite fine. Put inside a bowl.
3. Add milk-soaked bread & the seasonings to the meat.
4. Stir thoroughly, then shape into meatballs that are 2-3 inches in diameter in the shape of footballs. Every skewer must be able to hold about 2 or 3 meatballs. These can be formed directly on the skewers.
5. Grill food on skewers up to thoroughly done.

36. LOW FAT MIDDLE EASTERN BEEF KOFTAS

Ready In:20mins

Ingredients:12

Serves:4

INGREDIENTS

- 450g lean ground beef
- 1 red onion
- 1 cup of mint
- 1/2 cup of fresh parsley
- 1 lemon
- 1/2 tsp pepper
- 1/2 tsp allspice
- 2 tsp cumin
- 2 tsp cori&er
- cooking spray
- 1 cup of non-fat vanilla yogurt
- 4 tbsp mint sauce

DIRECTIONS

1. GRATED lemon rind, GRATED red onion, parsley, mint, allspice, & beef must all be combined in a bowl.
2. Make 7 or 8 rolled sausages in total.
3. Cook beef in an oiled pan up to done.
4. NOTE: Rolling the sausages uniformly will make cooking easier.
5. NOTE: To help the top brown evenly, I added a plate & a can from the pantry.
6. Combine vanilla low-fat yogurt & mint sauce in a separate bowl (I used from the bottle; thick or thin will do).
7. Will serve with grape tomatoes & the spiced pumpkin recipe from Bill Granger that is on ZAAR!
8. ENJOY!
9. **
10. UPDATE: Add up to 2 tbsp of Greek yogurt if the mixture FEELS dry. If the mixture is too dry before grilling, it will also taste that way.

37. BEEF KOFTAS WITH MINTED YOGURT

Ready In: 35mins

Ingredients: 13

Serves: 4

INGREDIENTS

- 1 cup of fresh parsley leaves, lightly packed
- 3 green onions, coarsely chop up

- 2 tsp dried mint
- 1/2 tsp ground cumin
- 1/2 tsp paprika
- 1/2 tsp salt
- 1/4 tsp pepper
- 1 egg
- 1 lb lean ground beef
- 1/2 cup of plain yogurt
- 2 tbsp fresh parsley, chop up
- 4 pita bread, whole wheat
- 2 tbsp water

DIRECTIONS

1. Combine the chop up parsley with the green onions, half the mint, cumin, paprika, salt, & pepper in a blender. Add to a big bowl & stir in the egg. Combine in the steak & 2 tbsp of water.
2. Form the meat mixture into little sausage shapes by putting 2 tbsp onto a metal skewer lengthwise.
3. Put the skewers on the grill over medium heat, close the lid, & cook, flipping once, for 12 mins, or up to the inside is no longer pink (or broil, turning once, for 7 mins).
4. While that is happening, blend yogurt with the remaining mint & parsley. Pitas must be heated through & lightly crisped on the grill or broiler for about 4 mins; then slice every one into quarters. Serve yogurt & pita cubes with the koftas.

38. CURRY BEEF SHORT RIBS WITH HORSERADISH SAUCE

Ready In: 2hrs

Ingredients: 13

Serves: 8

INGREDIENTS

- 3 lbs short rib of beef
- 1/4 cup of flour
- 2 tsp salt
- 1/2 tsp pepper
- 2 tbsp olive oil or 2 tbsp vegetable oil

- 2 medium onions, split
- 1 tbsp Worcestershire sauce
- 1 - 1 1/2 tsp curry powder
- 1 tsp molasses or 1 tsp maple syrup
- 1/2 tsp gingerroot, chop up
- 1 cup of water
- 1 cup of sour cream
- 2 tbsp horseradish

DIRECTIONS

1. Set the oven to 350°F.
2. Combine the pepper, salt, & flour. Lightly dust the beef short ribs with the flour mixture.
3. Beef short ribs must be well-browned on both sides in a big saute pan that has been heated to medium-high heat with 2 T of oil. Do in groups. Take out & place aside.
4. Onions, Worcestershire sauce, curry, molasses, water, & ginger must be combined in a sizable baking dish with a lid or roasting pan with foil. In the mixture, add the beef short ribs, & tightly cover. 1 1/2 to 2 hours of baking.
5. Take out of the oven, then standard for a few mins. Combine horseradish & sour cream in a mini bowl.
6. With a horseradish & sour cream sauce, serve the beef short ribs.
7. Itadakimasu!

39. SLOW-COOKED BEEF SHORT RIBS WITH RED WINE SAUCE

Ready In:6hrs 25mins

Ingredients:15

Serves:6

INGREDIENTS

- 2 tbsp flour
- 1 tsp salt
- 1/8 tsp ground black pepper
- 4 lbs beef short ribs
- 2 tbsp extra virgin olive oil
- 2 onions, split
- 1 cup of red wine

- 1 cup of chili sauce
- 6 tbsp brown sugar
- 6 tbsp apple cider vinegar
- 2 tbsp Worcestershire sauce
- 1 tsp dry mustard
- 1 tsp chili powder
- 4 tbsp flour
- 1/2 cup of red wine

DIRECTIONS

1. Combine flour, salt, & pepper. Apply the mixture on the ribs.
2. Brown the short ribs all over in a big skillet with medium-high heat & olive oil.
3. Onions, 1 cup of red wine, chili sauce, brown sugar, vinegar, Worcestershire, dry mustard, & chili powder are all combined in a crock pot. the mixture with the ribs.
4. Cook for 6 hours with the cover off.
5. Place the ribs on a dish & reheat.
6. Remaining flour & red wine are added, then the crockpot is set to high. Simmer for 10 mins, or up to the sauce is well combineed & thickened.
7. Serve the ribs right away after pouring on the sauce!

40. BRAISED BEEF SHORT RIBS WITH A BORDELAISE SAUCE

Ready In:3hrs 45mins

Ingredients:10

Yields:4ribs

Serves:2

INGREDIENTS

- 4beef short ribs
- 1 cup of diced carrot
- 1 cup of diced celery
- 1 cup of diced onion
- 1 tbsp fresh garlic, chop up
- 1 tbsp fresh thyme
- 1(6 oz) can tomato paste

- 2 cups of red wine, Edmeades Zinf&el preferred
- 2 tbsp peppercorns
- 1 1/2 quarts beef stock

DIRECTIONS

1. Heat a sizzling hot big saute pan. I use sea salt & freshly ground pepper to season the ribs on both sides. Ribs must be seared for 1-2 mins on every side in 1 tbsp of olive oil. Take out of the pan & put in a big casserole dish. All vegetables, thyme, & peppercorns must be sauteed for 5 mins over medium heat. Tomato paste must be added & thoroughly combineed in, with no lumps. Using red wine as a deglazer, simmer for five mins to decrease. Bring to a boil after adding beef stock. The ribs must be covered & broiled for three hours at 325 Ds with all the sauce.
2. After done, take out the ribs & keep them warm. Save 3/4 cup of the sauce after straining the vegetables, then put the pot back on medium high heat. To gently thicken the remaining sauce, combine equal parts of cold water & flour into the saved sauce. When finished, dish the ribs & spoon the sauce over them. I served this with steamed baby carrots & garlic mashed potatoes.

41. SMOKED BEEF RIBS WITH DEVIL SAUCE

Ready In: 5hrs 30mins

Ingredients 14

Serves: 8

INGREDIENTS

- 5-6lbs beef ribs
- 1/3 cup of kosher salt
- 1/3 cup of brown sugar
- 2 tbsp course ground black pepper
- 1 tbsp grated lemon zest
- 2 tsp Tabasco sauce
- 1 cup of beef broth
- 1/2 cup of Worcestershire sauce
- 1/3 cup of cider vinegar
- 1/3 cup of vegetable oil
- 1 tsp dry mustard
- 1 tsp chili powder

- 1 tsp paprika
- 3 tsp Tabasco sauce

DIRECTIONS

1. Combine the first six marinade ingredients. the ribs' backs must be free of rough skin. Rub & marinate.
2. over the ribs on both sides.
3. Overnight marinate covered.
4. The next 6 ingredients must be combined in a sauce pan & brought to a boil.
5. to warm the ribs up.
6. Place in smoker & cook for 45 mins per lb of meat at 225°F.
7. every time you put wood in, mop with sauce.

42. BEEF RIBS WITH CABERNET SAUCE

Ready In:2hrs 30mins

Ingredients11

Serves:4

INGREDIENTS

- 2 tsp dried marjoram
- 2 tsp paprika
- 1 tsp granulated garlic
- 1 tsp light brown sugar
- 1 tsp kosher salt
- 1 tsp fresh ground black pepper
- MEAT
- 2beef baby back rib racks, about 5 pounds
- SAUCE
- 1 1/2 cups of barbecue sauce
- 1 cup of cabernet sauvignon wine
- OTHER INGREDIENTS
- kosher salt
- fresh ground black pepper

DIRECTIONS

1. It's a good idea to have a backup plan in case the main one fails.

2. Slice off any extra fat from the ribs; rub the rub into the meat; cover with plastic wrap; & chill for 8 to 12 hours.
3. Before grilling, let ribs to sit at room temperature for 20–30 mins.
4. Around 10 mins of even browning can be achieved by searing over direct medium heat while turning once halfway through.
5. If necessary, chop the ribs into smaller pieces before transferring to a heavy-gauge aluminum pan big enough to contain the ribs in one layer.
6. To prepare the sauce, combine the ingredients in a pot & heat them up to boiling.
7. After covering the ribs with aluminum foil, drizzle the sauce over them.
8. Grill the ribs over indirect medium heat up to extremely tender, 1 ½ to 2 hours, flipping once halfway through grilling time.
9. Slice the ribs into single or double-rib pieces after removing them from the pan.
10. Serve the ribs hot with the sauce on the side & skim any fat from the sauce before seasoning with salt & pepper.

43. BEEF SHORT RIBS WITH BARBECUE SAUCE

Ready In: 2hrs 55mins

Ingredients: 10

Serves: 6

INGREDIENTS

- 3 lbs beef short ribs
- 1 1/2 tsp salt
- 1/2 cup of water
- 1/2 cup of onion, chop up
- 2 garlic cloves, chop up
- 1 (6 oz) can tomato paste
- 1 cup of ketchup
- 3/4 cup of brown sugar, firmly packed
- 1/2 cup of apple cider vinegar
- 2 tbsp prepared mustard (not dry)

DIRECTIONS

1. Brown the shortribs all over in a sizable skillet (without any oil or shortening), cover, & cook at a low temperature for an hour before draining the pan drippings.
2. The remaining sauce components must be combined.
3. Shortribs must be covered snugly in sauce & cooked for an additional 1 1/2 hours at a low temperature (or up to meat is tender).

44. VEGGIES & CHICKEN & VEGGIES

Ready In: 20mins

Ingredients: 15

Serves: 4

INGREDIENTS

- 2 tbsp olive oil
- 1 lb boneless skinless chicken breast (slice in thin strips)
- 1 medium onion, split
- 1 pint grape tomatoes, smashed
- 2 cups of broccoli, in bite size florets
- 1 cup of red bell pepper, slice into strips
- 1 cup of green bell pepper, slice into strips
- 1 cup of yellow squash, split
- 1 cup of zucchini, split
- 2 garlic cloves, split
- 1/2 cup of Wondra Flour
- 3/4 cup of dry white wine (chardonnay)
- 3/4 cup of chicken broth
- 2 tbsp fresh basil, chop up
- salt & pepper

DIRECTIONS

1. Chicken strips must be salt & pepper-seasoned.
2. Cook the chicken in 1 tbsp of oil in a big skillet up to it is well-browned & done.
3. Chicken must be taken out & set aside.
4. Add the remaining olive oil to the pan & start sautéing the vegetables according to the instructions.

5. Reintroduce the chicken to the pan & sprinkle with flour after all the vegetables are crisp-tender.
6. Add flour to the pan's contents.
7. Stir in the wine & broth up to thickened.
8. Lastly, season with salt & pepper as need.
9. Serve with potatoes, spaghetti, or rice.

45. PAN ROASTED CHICKEN & VEGGIES

Ready In:1hr 5mins

Ingredients:9

Serves:4

INGREDIENTS

- 1 1/2 lbs red potatoes, slice into 1 1/2-inch chunks
- 1 big onion, slice into wedges
- 4 garlic cloves
- 2 tbsp olive oil
- 1 1/4 tsp salt
- 1/2 tsp black pepper
- 1/2 tsp dried rosemary
- 1 lb boneless skinless chicken thighs, every slice in quarters
- 1(10 oz) bag fresh spinach (take out stems)

DIRECTIONS

1. Set the oven to 475 °F.
2. Combine potatoes, onion, garlic, oil, salt, pepper, & rosemary in a sizable roasting pan & toss to coat.
3. 25 mins of roasting, once stirring.
4. Chicken must be lightly salted & peppered before being added, coated, & roasted for a further 15 mins or up to done.
5. Put spinach on top of the chicken mixture & roast for an additional five mins, or up to the spinach wilts.
6. Before serving, toss.

46. VA VOOM VEGGIE BURGERS

Ready In:27mins

Ingredients:7

Yields:5patties

INGREDIENTS

- 1 cup of cooked pureed white beans, including some liquid or 1 cup of beans, of your choice (try Bush's baked vegetarian beans!)
- 1 cup of cooked brown rice (try yellow rice!)
- 1/2 cup of uncooked quaker multigrain cereal (or oats)
- 1 cup of cornbread stuffing combine (Pepperidge Farm is good)
- 1 tbsp parsley
- 1/2 cup of chop up onion
- 1 tbsp soy sauce

DIRECTIONS

1. Combine all ingredients.
2. Incorporate patties.
3. Fry up to every side is browned over low heat in olive oil.
4. Serve on a bun with your preferred toppings, including lettuce, tomato, & grilled onions.
5. Enjoy!

47. EASY VEGGIE BURGERS

Ready In:13mins

Ingredients:13

Serves:6

INGREDIENTS

- 19ozs black beans
- 1/3 cup of onion, coarsely chop up
- 1 garlic clove, chop up
- 1 egg
- 3 tbsp barbecue sauce or 3 tbsp ketchup
- 11 tbsp soya sauce or 1 1/2 tsp HP steak sauce
- 1 tsp canola oil
- 1/2 tsp salt

- 1/2 tsp pepper, freshly ground
- 1/3 cup of all-purpose flour
- 1/2 cup of dry breadcrumbs (must be store bought to work) or 1/2 cup of cracker crumb, ground in processor up to very fine (must be store bought to work)
- 1/2 cup of old cheddar cheese, shredded
- 6crusty bread rolls

DIRECTIONS

1. Beans must be drained & washed in cold water.
2. Drain once more, then use paper towels to dry.
3. To a mixer, add beans, onions, garlic, egg, 2 tbsp barbecue sauce, Worcestershire sauce, oil, salt, & pepper.
4. Beans must be pulsed up to they are pea-sized.
5. Add the blended ingredients to a big bowl.
6. Add the flour & blend thoroughly.
7. Combine in the bread crumbs thoroughly.
8. Including cheese, combine with your hands (mixture is thick).
9. Create six equal amounts of the mixture.
10. To make 1/2-inch thick burgers, flour your hands first because the batter would adhere to them otherwise.
11. The burgers can be refrigerate up to you're ready to grill them, or they can be chilled in a covered container for 1 day.
12. Pre-heat the grill to medium-high & oil it.
13. Put hamburgers on the grill.
14. Brush on any leftover barbeque sauce.
15. For 8 to 10 mins, grill with the lid down up to the food is hot & turn it once.
16. Serve on buns with chosen toppings i.e. pickles, onions, tomatoes, salsa.
17. Use soy sauce or a vegetarian Worcestershire sauce if you're a vegetarian.

48. COOL VEGGIE PIZZA

Ready In:1hr

Ingredients:7

Serves:10

INGREDIENTS

- 1(8 oz) box/pkg refrigerated crescent dinner rolls
- 1(8 oz) box/pkg cream cheese, dilute
- 1 1/2 tsp mayonnaise

- 1 clove pressed garlic
- 1 tsp dried dill weed
- salt & pepper
- 2 cups of assorted fresh vegetables, chop up (any combination, e.g. broccoli, green onions, bell peppers, mushrooms, carrots, & tomatoes)

DIRECTIONS

1. the oven to 350 Ds.
2. Place the unrolled crescent rolls on a sizable baking sheet.
3. To seal seams, press.
4. Bake for 12 to 15 mins, or up to golden.
5. Complete cooling.
6. Combine well the remaining ingredients, EXCEPT the veggies.
7. On the crust's top, evenly distribute the cream cheese mixture.
8. Top the crust with chop up vegetables.
9. At least 30 mins or up to a day in advance, cover & chill.
10. Before serving, slice the cake into mini squares.

49. PASTA WITH SAUSAGE, TOMATOES, & CREAM

Ready In: 25mins

Ingredients: 11

Serves: 2

INGREDIENTS

- 1 tbsp olive oil
- 1/2 lb sweet Italian sausage link, casings take outd, cut up
- 1/4 tsp crushed dried red pepper flakes
- 1/4 cup of diced onion
- 1 1/2 cloves garlic, chop up
- 1 (14 1/2 oz) can Italian plum tomatoes, drained, coarsely chop up
- 3/4 cup of whipping cream
- 1/4 tsp salt
- 6 ozs pasta
- 1 1/2 tbsp chop up parsley
- grated parmesan cheese

DIRECTIONS

1. In a big skillet over medium heat, warm the oil.
2. Add sausage & red pepper flakes.
3. Sauté up to sausage is no longer pink, stirring regularly, about 7 mins.
4. Stirring occasionally, add the onion & garlic to the skillet & simmer for about 7 mins, or up to the onion is soft & the sausage is lightly browned.
5. Add salt, cream, & tomatoes.
6. Simmer for 4 mins or up to mixture slightly thickens.
7. (May be made a day in advance. Cover & let it rest.).
8. In a big pot of boiling water, cook pasta.
9. Drain.
10. Simmering the sauce.
11. Pasta must be added to the sauce & cooked for 2 mins, stirring regularly, up to pasta is thoroughly warm & the sauce has thickened.
12. Distribute the pasta among plates.
13. Add parsley as a garnish.
14. Pass the Parmesan separately as you serve.

50. TURKEY BREAKFAST SAUSAGE PATTIES

Ready In: 15mins

Ingredients: 12

Serves: 4-6

INGREDIENTS

- 1 lb ground turkey
- 1 tsp salt
- 2 tsp sage
- 1 tsp fennel seed
- 1 tsp thyme
- 1 tsp black pepper
- 1/2 tsp white pepper
- 1/2 tsp cayenne
- 1/4 tsp garlic powder
- 1/8 tsp ground cloves
- 1/8 tsp nutmeg
- 1/8 tsp allspice

DIRECTIONS

1. If you don't want a spicy flavor, use less pepper when combining all the ingredients together.
2. If you have the time, let the meat sit in the refrigerator overnight to let the spices flavor the flesh.
3. Create patties, cook as needed, & freeze any extras.
4. Avoid overcooking them or they will dry out; take them off the heat as soon as the insides are no longer pink but the outsides are still juicy. (if you prefer a moister texture, you add a dash of olive oil or an egg to the mixture immediately prior to cooking).

51. EGGS BAKED IN BACON RING

Ready In:20mins

Ingredients:4

Serves:6

INGREDIENTS

- 6slices bacon
- 6 eggs
- salt & pepper
- dilute butter

DIRECTIONS

1. the oven to 325 Ds.
2. Lightly broil or saute bacon strips.
3. Butter must be used to coat the muffin pan's bottom.
4. The bacon is used to line the sides.
5. Put one egg in every dish.
6. Eggs must be baked for 10 mins or up to done.
7. Turn them out onto pineapple rings, rounds of bread, or English muffins.

52. GREEN BEANS IN CHEESY BACON SAUCE (CROCK POT)

Ready In:5hrs 10mins

Ingredients:8

Serves:8-10

INGREDIENTS

- 2(16 oz) box/pkgs refrigerate slice green beans (I used fresh that we put in the freezer last summer)
- 1/2 cup of lightly chop up onion
- 1(4 oz) jar split pimiento, drained
- 1(4 oz) can split mushrooms, drained
- 1(10 3/4 oz) can condensed cream of mushroom soup
- 1 1/2 cups of shredded cheddar cheese (about 6 oz)
- 1/4 tsp pepper
- 6slices bacon, crisp-cooked, drained & cut up

DIRECTIONS

1. Combine green beans, onion, pimiento, mushrooms, soup, cheese, & pepper in a 3 1/2 to 4 quart crock pot.
2. Bacon crumbs must be sprinkled on top.
3. Cook with the lid on for 4–5 hours on low or 2 1/2–3 hours on high.
4. Before serving, stir.

53. ASPARAGUS WRAPPED IN BACON

Ready In:30mins

Ingredients:4

Serves:4-5

INGREDIENTS

- 1 lb asparagus (washed)
- extra virgin olive oil
- 6slices bacon
- salt & pepper

DIRECTIONS

1. Trim the asparagus's end to a length of between 1/2 & 1 inch.

2. It must have a minimum length of 4 to 5 inches.
3. Olive oil must only be used to lightly coat the asparagus. A little salt & pepper must also be used (non-compulsory).
4. Asparagus must be separated into bundles of about four, & every bundle must have one piece of raw bacon wrapped around it starting at the bottom.
5. Repeat for the remainder.
6. Put on broiler pan & bake for 5 mins at 500 Ds; then, flip them over & bake for an additional 5 mins.
7. Bake for 15 to 20 mins after lowering oven temperature to 350 Ds.

54. SLOW-COOKER BEEF SHORT RIBS

Ready In: 9hrs 10mins

Ingredients: 14

Serves: 6

INGREDIENTS

- 1/3 cup of flour
- 1 tsp salt
- 1/4 tsp pepper
- 2 1/2 lbs boneless beef short ribs
- 1/4 cup of butter
- 1 cup of chop up onion
- 1 cup of beef broth
- 3/4 cup of red wine vinegar
- 3/4 cup of brown sugar
- 1/4 cup of chili sauce
- 2 tbsp catsup
- 2 tbsp Worcestershire sauce
- 2 tbsp chop up garlic
- 1 tsp chili powder

DIRECTIONS

1. Fill a bag with flour, salt, & pepper.
2. Add the ribs, then shake to coat.
3. Butter-brown ribs in a big skillet.
4. Add to a slow cooker.
5. Combine the remaining ingredients in the same skillet.

Made in the USA
Columbia, SC
23 December 2023